Safari

Gail Tuchman

NATIONAL GEOGRAPHIC

Washington, D.C.

For Lauren—with love on your "journey."
—G.T.

Published by the National Geographic Society. Washington, D.C. 20036. All rights reserved.
Reproduction in whole or in part without written permission of the publisher is strictly prohibited.

Library of Congress Cataloging-in-Publication Data
Tuchman, Gail.
Safari / Gail Tuchman.
p. cm.
ISBN 978-1-4263-0614-3 (pbk. : alk. paper) -- ISBN 978-1-4263-0615-0 (library binding : alk. paper)
1. Animals--Africa--Juvenile literature. 2. Safaris--Africa--Juvenile literature. I. Title.
QL336.T83 2010
591.96--dc22
2009022830

Printed in the United States of America

cover, Beverly Joubert/ NationalGeographicStock.com; 1, Panoramic Images/ Getty Images; 2, Eric Isselée/ Shutterstock; 3, Remi Benali/ Corbis; 4-5, Remi Benali/Corbis; 6, WorldFoto/ Alamy/ Alamy; 11, Dave Hamman/ Gallo Images/ Getty Images; 8-9, Karine Aigner/ NationalGeographicStock.com; 12, Mitsuaki Iwago/ Minden Pictures/ NationalGeographicStock.com; 13 top, James Warwick/ The Image Bank/ Getty Images; 13 bottom left, D7INAMI7S/ Shutterstock; 13 bottom right, Michael Nichols/ NationalGeographicStock.com; 14-15, Panoramic Images/ Getty Images; 16, Bobby Model/ NationalGeographicStock.com; 19, Mitsuaki Iwago/ Minden Pictures; 20 top right, ZSSD/ Minden Pictures; 20 bottom left, D7INAMI7S/ Shutterstock; 20 bottom right, Mitsuaki Iwago/ NationalGeographicStock.com; 20 top right, Suzi Eszterhas/ Minden Pictures; 21 right, Kletr/ Shutterstock; 22-23, Matrin Harvey/ Foto Natura/ Minden Pictures/ NationalGeographicStock.com; 24, Norbert Rosing/ NationalGeographicStock.com; 21 left, George F. Mobley/ NationalGeographicStock.com; Hippo illustrations by Dan Sipple.

11/WOR/4

Hello! **Jambo!**
Let's go.

I'm going on safari.

What will I see?

I see elephants spray,
just for me.

I see elephants spray,
on safari.

I see lions play,
just for me.

I see lions play,
on safari.

I see rhinos run,
just for me.

I see rhinos run,
on safari.

Rhinos run.
Lions play.
Elephants spray.

What else will
I see on safari?

I see giraffes eat,
just for me.

I see giraffes eat,
on safari.

I see zebras graze, just for me.

I see zebras graze, on safari.

I see hippos soak,
just for me.

I see hippos soak,
on safari.

Hippos soak.
Zebras graze.
Giraffes eat.
Rhinos run.
Lions play.
Elephants spray.

What else will I see?

I see animals all around me...

on safari!